How to Love IT More and Hate IT Less

A Business Owner's Guide to Less IT Frustration and Worry

Jim Hood
Intellis
P.O. Box 2068
Petaluma, CA 94953-2068
jhood@intellis-tech.com
www.intellis-tech.com

Table of Contents

Introduction

I have heard it time and time again from my customers...."it's a love-hate relationship with my computers!!" One of my most popular IT marketing giveaways was a 5½" foam hammer that could be used for computer bashing! It gave some needed relief.

Of course, this is serious business. As a business owner, your business depends on your IT systems. Let's look at some industry studies.

- A survey of 900 business users across North America, Europe and Asia found that 86% of employees lose an average of 18 hours a month-totaling more than 200 hours each year per employee-due to IT issues and the subsequent challenges in resolving them. This represents an average annual cost of approximately $3,700 per employee. Some employees spike at much higher losses. (Forrester Survey, April 2013)
- 25% of small-to-mid-sized businesses will suffer a major disaster causing loss of critical data every 5 years. (Richmond House Group)
- 70% of small firms that experience a major data loss go out of business within a year. (Contingency Planning, Strategic Research Corp., and DTI/Price Waterhouse Coopers, 2004)
- Companies that experience a computer outage lasting greater than 10 days will never fully recover financially. (Jon Toiga, Disaster Recovery Planning: Managing Risk & Catastrophe in Information Systems, Yourdon Press 1989)

- Companies report an average of over 500 hours of network downtime every year and overall, downtime costs an average of 3.6% of annual revenue. (Infonetics Research)

The financial impact of the lost productivity due to IT issues is staggering.

As a small business owner, you can't afford losing more than 200 hours per year per employee in lost productivity, and a loss of critical data could put you out of business.

If your computers or network goes down, we know how critically important it is to get you back up and running quickly. Our goal is to head off problems with our proactive managed services programs before the problems get to be big and expensive with extensive down time.

This guide is intended to help you better understand IT systems and solutions, help prevent the extremely expensive loss of productivity, and the very real risk of losing your business from a loss of critical data. As much as possible, the use of techno-babble has been minimized. We have tried to write this guide for you, the business owner, who has plenty to do running the business instead of spending time on technical IT issues.

We at Intellis are committed to helping you select the right IT systems and solutions, reduce lost productivity, secure your IT systems, and reduce the risk of data loss as your trusted IT partner.

And finally, a good indication that that there is more love, and less hate, with your IT system is if you are using the computer bashing hammer less!

Chapter 1: The Basics That Must Be In Place

1.1 Anti-malware Protection

Malware is a generic term that includes viruses, spyware, Trojan Horses, bots, relays, and other terms. There must be anti-virus and anti-spyware software installed on all computers and the anti-virus/spyware definitions must be automatically updating regularly. The definitions contain information about the malware that lets the software detect and eliminate them. Anti-virus software products usually also include anti-spyware, and other anti-malware components. *If the paid subscription for the anti-virus/anti-spyware programs lapses, the definitions won't be updated and the computers will be vulnerable.* It is critically important to keep the subscriptions current. While no anti-malware program can guarantee you won't be infected by malware, it is critically important to have anti-malware software installed on your computers.

There are many different anti-malware software products available. Some products offer basic, essential anti-virus and anti-spyware protection, but not firewalls, identity protection, and other protection modules. The basic, essential products are usually the least intrusive on your use of the computer. They usually stay out of sight and don't slow the computer down. The more fully featured products, frequently called "Internet Security", can be frustrating if their firewall blocks Internet access to some sites, and the programs sometimes take a significant percentage of the processor's capability, resulting in a sluggish computer.

Usually, the basic, essential products provide sufficient protection. For example, Microsoft Security Essentials and Microsoft Defender are free anti-virus/anti-spyware programs offering good basic protection. Because it does not include a firewall, the computer's operating system firewall must be used.

Sometimes, programs that only check your computer for installed anti-virus/anti-spyware programs and firewalls are downloaded and installed. McAfee Security Scan is an example. *These are not anti-virus/anti-spyware programs and will not protect you.* All these programs do is check to see if you have anti-malware programs installed.

Anti-virus/anti-spyware programs protect against viruses and spyware. However, there are other types of malware that the anti-virus/anti-spyware programs sometimes won't detect. An example of a complementary program to the anti-virus/anti-spyware programs to protect against the malware that the major anti-virus programs sometimes miss is Malwarebytes.

To provide the most complete protection, we usually install both an anti-virus/anti-spyware program and a program like Malwarebytes.

Unfortunately, viruses and other malware are becoming more vicious, and increasingly difficult to remove from the computer. Loss of data, corruption of the operating system, and loss of use of the computer can result from an infection. Frequently, it is necessary to reformat the computer's hard drive and reload all software and data, which is time consuming and expensive. If data had not been backed up before the infection, it may not be possible to recover the data.

Intellis can install and check your anti-malware programs and make sure they are fully functional. Through our 24x7 remote managed service solutions, we provide complete management of your anti-malware protection. We install the programs, verify that the anti-malware programs are running, and the definitions are updating regularly.

Precautions

1. Always have anti-virus/anti-spyware and compatible complementary anti-malware programs installed with current subscriptions and definitions that are being updated regularly.
2. Don't open email attachments from unknown senders. Even official looking emails from senders like major banks, USPS, and other institutions may be fakes with viruses in the attachments. It's best not to even open the email itself. Delete these items.
3. Even emails appearing to be from known senders can be fraudulent. Be very careful about opening any attachment.
4. Be very careful where you go on the Internet. Some links will infect your computer when you access the site. If you think you have been hit by a virus from accessing a site, disconnect your Internet cable or turn off your Wi-Fi connection as quickly as possible. This may prevent even more viruses from coming into the computer.
5. If you receive a warning that your computer has been infected by a virus, do not click on any links to purchase and download programs to get rid of the infections. These are scams that infect your computer in the first place and then try to collect money from you for a download that will not get rid of the infections.

1.2 Backups and Disaster Recovery

There are many types of disasters that can strike: earthquakes, fire, flood, theft, sabotage, accidental damage, accidental employee error, viruses, and equipment failure.

San Fernando, CA Earthquake

Your business data is too critical to be vulnerable to disasters. In addition to a comprehensive backup solution, you need a disaster recovery plan with step-by-step instructions for how to recover your data.

Many small businesses start by manually backing up their data to an external hard drive, DVD, or flash drive. This is better than no backup, but this is not a complete backup solution. All hard drives will eventually fail. Fortunately, today most hard drives will last many years without failures, but we are talking statistics here, and there is a percentage of hard drives that aren't going to last many years. You have lost your backup data if your external hard drive fails or is stolen or damaged by a disaster. DVD's can be scratched or cracked. Flash drives can be lost or stolen. If a manual approach is used, the backups can take lower priority when things get busy, and frequently aren't done.

The best backup solution combines local external backup media with offsite storage and automated backup software. The local external backup media, usually a hard drive or network attached storage (NAS) appliance, allows fast data recovery if the hard drive in your computer fails. If the local external backup drive fails, is stolen, or destroyed in a disaster, the offsite backup can be retrieved. Reputable cloud data backup companies today have replicated data location centers in different parts of the country, encrypted data communication links between your facility and the backup location, and encrypt your data that is stored in their facility. Data redundancy within their storage locations takes the risk out of their own hard drives failing.

A written disaster recovery plan will allow you to quickly recover your data in the chaos that usually accompanies a major disaster. It won't rely on a particular IT support individual who has all the information, who may or may not be reachable. It will contain a description of what data is backup up, where the data is located, account numbers and passwords, contact information, and step-by-step instructions for getting the data back.

What if you lose critical data, either from accidently deleting it, or from a disk failure and you don't have a backup? Intellis has a data recovery system in our office that can frequently recover user data that has been deleted, or from a failed disk. However, if the damage to the disk is too extensive, we may not be able to recover the data, and we may not be able to recover all deleted files. If this is the case, we can send the disk drive to a professional data recovery lab where clean room technology, and sophisticated recovery techniques usually can get your data back. We will work with you to get your data back if it is at all possible.

Intellis can set up a complete backup solution for you and write your disaster recovery plan. With our 24x7 proactive managed services programs, we monitor the results of each of your backups and will know if a backup fails. If we cannot fix the issue remotely, we contact you to make arrangements for fixing the problem. If a disaster strikes, we can get your data back and get you up and running as quickly as possible.

Precautions

1. Protect your data with a local backup drive or NAS appliance *and* offsite storage in a professional data center.
2. Make sure the cloud data storage company you use has been an established business for a significant period of time with good reviews, and uses encryption for the communication links as well as the data storage.
3. Have a written disaster recovery plan.
4. Keep the software CD/DVD's and software product keys for your computers in a safe location so they can be quickly accessed if it is ever necessary to reformat your computer hard drives, or replace hard drives, and reload all software. If you don't have the CD/DVD's, they can sometimes be purchased or downloaded from the manufacturers.

1.3 Security

Bodiam Castle, England

There are layers of security, and we will start with the outer layer, which is usually your router with built-in firewall and other protection, or a hardware firewall unit with built-in router and other protection. The router's job is to join the wide area (e.g. the ISP network) and local area (e.g. your premise network) networks together. Many businesses successfully use a router, such as Cisco, Linksys, Netgear, D-Link or other devices, that has a built-in firewall, network address translation, and packet inspection capability as the first line of defense for their network. These router capabilities are intended to stop hackers from accessing your network. The firewall, network address translation (NAT), and state packet inspection (SPI) thwart intruders and must be enabled in the router.

If additional protection and capability are needed, there are hardware firewalls, such as SonicWALL devices, that integrate intrusion prevention, malware protection, and virtual private network (VPN) interfaces into the router. The choice of firewall/router will depend on your network and applications.

The next layer is provided by your server, or if there is no server, your computers. The server/computers must have a firewall that is enabled, and anti-malware protection, even with the firewall (and anti-malware in some firewall/routers) enabled in the outer layer of protection.

In addition to intrusion protection provided by your network equipment and server/computers, you must do your part with effective passwords. Your computer logon must be password protected. Create passwords that have at least 6 alphanumeric characters, and preferably 8, and are not names that someone could obtain from public records about you or your business. Change your password regularly.

Phishing is someone trying to acquire information from you over the Internet such as usernames, passwords, credit card information, and sometimes money, by pretending to be a trusted source. Communications supposedly from government organizations, popular social web sites, auction sites, banks, online payment processors or IT administrators are commonly used to fool you. Phishing emails may contain links to websites infected with malware. Phishing is typically carried out by email spoofing or instant messaging, and it often directs users to enter details at a fake website whose look and feel are almost identical to the legitimate one. The best defense is educating your employees to be aware of phishing attacks, and never give out this type of information over the Internet.

There are other types of security breaches, such as the ones caused by bots (short for robots) and botnets, relays, and others that should be taken out by your anti-malware programs. In addition to keeping the anti-malware programs updating the malware definitions, it is important to keep your operating system software updated with security updates. Windows Automatic Updates and Mac Software Update for your computers should be enabled and in use.

Sometimes there will be data so sensitive and critical to the business that you will want to encrypt it on your hard drive.

Encrypting hard drives, folders and files is a way to protect them from unwanted access. Encrypting File System (EFS) is a feature of Windows 7 Professional and Ultimate that allows you to store information on your hard disk in an encrypted format. Apple Mac systems can use Disk Utility to encrypt files. The first time you encrypt a folder or file, you should back up your encryption certificate. If your certificate and key are lost or damaged and you do not have a backup, you won't be able to use the files that you have encrypted. Third party encryption programs are also available.

Remember, if you lose the encryption key you create, your data cannot be retrieved……it's gone.

Precautions

1. Do not turn off the firewalls in your router, firewall appliance, server, or computers. If they are blocking sites you need to access, the firewalls can be configured to allow access to these sites.
2. Do not turn off other default settings in your router or firewall appliance such as NAT or SPI.
3. Always have strong passwords for your computer logon, web email accounts, and other personal accounts. Change them frequently.
4. Never give personal information such as social security number, credit card information, username, passwords out over the Internet in response to requests from any agency or person. If you use credit cards to make purchases over the Internet, make sure the Internet merchant is reputable, well known, and the link in use is encrypted.

5. Do not turn off automatic updates of your software. These updates are needed to keep your system secure. Applications such as Adobe Acrobat, Reader and Flash Player, QuickTime, Skype, and others may need to be manually updated. Frequently, there is an Update link in the Help menu.
6. Encrypt sensitive data on your hard drive with either the built-in file and folder encryption capability of your computer's operating system, or third party encryption programs. Remember, if you lose the encryption key used to encrypt the data, the data is lost forever.

1.4 Power Outage and Surge Protection

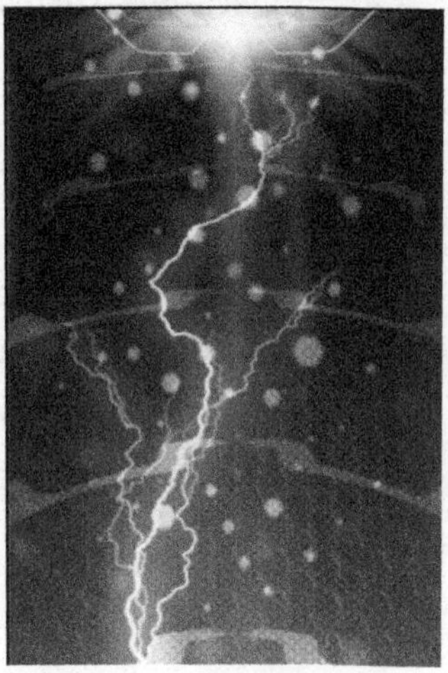

Power outages and surges while the computer is running can corrupt operating system and data files. This can result in loss of your data, computer crashes, and erratic behavior. Pulling your computer's power plug from the wall outlet while the computer is running can do the same thing. While there is generally more protection within the computer when pushing in on the front panel power button until the computer powers off, this should not be done except as a last resort to shut down the computer. The software should be used to shut down the computer if possible.

The best protection against power outages and surges is to use a battery backup uninterruptable power supply (UPS), such as APC's Back-UPS series. The batteries in these units will allow your computer to run off the batteries if the main AC electrical power fails. The units also have built-in surge protection. The units can also shut off your computer safely as the end of the battery life approaches after a power outage to avoid file damage when the UPS shuts down. The power capacity of the UPS needs to be matched to the power requirements of your computer system. The batteries in the UPS units need to be replaced every few years and this is a very important maintenance item.

In the absence of a UPS, at least a surge protected power strip should be used. This will not protect against software file corruption in the event of a power outage, but it will protect the computer from damage caused by power surges.

Precautions

1. Never unplug the computer power cord from the wall power outlet while the computer is running.
2. Avoid pushing in and holding the power button on the front panel of the computer as a way of powering off the computer except as a last resort.
3. Always shut off the computer using the computer software.
4. Best practice is to use a battery backup Uninterruptable Power Supply (UPS) to power your computer, and configure the setup so the UPS will shut off your computer safely if the battery backup time expires.
5. As a minimum, use a surge protected power strip for your computer. This is not necessary if a UPS is in use.

1.5 How Long Should I Keep My Computers?

Another frequent question is, "how long should I keep my computers?" To answer this, you have to start with what type of computers were purchased in the first place.

Computers tend to fall into four categories. The first is the consumer class. Price is very sensitive, and these computers typically do not get used in a business-critical environment. Most computers sold in discount retail stores fall into this category. To drive the price down, manufacturers drive the cost of components in the computer down. In general, the reliability and life of these computers will be less than business-class devices. The consumer class computers typically do not have the versions of operating system software installed that will allow them to fully join server networks, so there will limitations in what they can do in server environments. There is other functionality, such as built-in file and folder encryption, that may not be part of the operating system. If you only plan on keeping the computer 2 or 3 years, a consumer class computer may be OK if you are not in a server environment or need functionality that is only provided in the business class operating systems.

The second category is the business-class computer. An example of a business-class computer is the Dell OptiPlex. These computers will cost more than the consumer-class computers because they are designed to be more reliable with a longer life. Typically, they have operating systems that allow them to be joined to server environments with full functionality. They may not have as powerful a graphics capability as some consumer computers because gaming is more closely associated with the consumer class computer, or the more powerful professional workstations that need the enhanced graphics for computer aided design, graphics design and layout, etc. A quality business-class computer should last 5 or 6 years.

The third category is the high powered workstations that are used for computer aided design, intensive computational work, and similar applications. These usually are more expensive than the business-class computers with a similar life.

The fourth category is special application computers, such as tablets, thin clients, keyboard-less computers, and similar devices. Their use tends to be driven by specific applications, rather than whether they are consumer oriented or business oriented. Depending on the quality of the materials designed into the devices, they may be suitable for critical business use.

Another factor in determining how long to keep the computers is the cost of repair and lost productivity as computers age. For example, a 2009 study released by J. Gold Associates, a technology analysis firm in Northborough, MA, concluded that business laptops used in the enterprise should not be kept longer than 3 years due to the repair and lost productivity costs of a machine older than 3 years. (There is no indication that the computers in this study were covered by a preventative maintenance program).

Intellis believes that using our proactive preventative maintenance program with quality, business-class computers will allow you to keep the machines 5 or 6 years or longer without incurring steep costs as the computers age. We are committed to keeping your computers running effectively for as long as possible.

Precautions

1. Buy business-class computers for your business, not consumer-class.
2. Use proactive, preventative maintenance programs for your computers to keep them running reliably and fast for as long as possible.

Chapter 2: Keeping Your Computer Healthy

The next most often heard comment from my customers after "it's a love-hate relationship", is "my computer is sick… it's a slug." Computers are like your car: preventative maintenance will help keep them running reliably and fast.

Slug

The maintenance steps described below can be done by you if you have the time and inclination. Usually, things get busy and the maintenance doesn't get done, and the slugs start coming out. Intellis proactive managed services take care of the maintenance steps needed to keep your computers healthy and snappy for you.

2.1 Anti-malware Scans

Earlier, the importance of having anti-malware protection and keeping the malware definitions updated was described. A good first step in a maintenance program is to manually run the anti-malware programs to make sure malware hasn't bypassed the protection. Intellis installs a "Tuneup Folder" on your desktop that contains the needed anti-malware programs, such as Malwarebytes and Spybot Search & Destroy with instructions on how to do the tune-up. Your main anti-virus program should also be run. Manually update the definitions before running the programs. It is usually safe to follow the recommendations of the anti-malware programs, such "quarantine infections" or "delete infections".

Malware can nest in layers. If the anti-malware scan uncovers problems, the scan must be run again after eliminating the uncovered infections until the scan results in no malware found.

2.2 Software Updates

Earlier it was noted how important it is to keep your software applications and operating system up to date. A good second step in the maintenance program is to manually do updates to make sure this has happened. While security is the primary reason for the updates, performance and reliability problems can result from software version incompatibility due to software that has not been updated.

It is also a good idea to update the driver software in your computer. Drivers are the layer of software between the hardware and the higher level operating system software, and let the higher level software communicate with hardware. This can be done with the Windows Device Manager utility or the Mac Software Update utility in the operating system.

2.3 Hard Drive Cleanup

If your hard drive gets too full, your computer will slow down and eventually stop. As a rule of thumb, your hard drive should have at least 15% free disk space. People prone to loading up the hard drive with music and video have learned this the hard way.

The next step is to uninstall any unneeded programs. Even if you aren't using these programs, parts of them frequently start when the computer starts up, and this can slow down the computer.

A word of caution about installing programs is needed. You don't want to install any more programs than you actually need and use. Frequently, when downloading and installing programs, you will have the option for additional programs to be installed at the same time, with the default checkmarks in place to install them. It requires close attention on your part to uncheck these boxes so they won't be installed.

The next step is to run cCleaner, which we put in the Tuneup Folder on your desktop. cCleaner is a free utility that removes unused files and Internet debris from the hard drive, cleans up online history and cookies, and cleans the computer's registry.

The next step is to use the operating system's disk clean up utility to clean up the hard drive. This will eliminate error reporting logs, dumps, and other system files that are not needed.

The next step is to defragment your hard drive. Over time, file content becomes located in distributed locations across the disk surface, and is not contiguous. This results in extra "seeks" (movement of the disk read/write electromechanical actuator), and this slows things down. Defragmentation relocates the file content so the data is contiguous and this will speed up disk performance, and the performance of the computer. The Windows operating system has a disk defragmentation tool. Mac systems must use a third party defragmentation tool, and Apple states that "you should not need to frequently defragment the computer's hard drive because the file system used on Mac computers is designed to work with a certain degree of fragmentation".

With solid state drives (SSD) instead of rotating hard drives it is best not to run defragmentation or optimization routines.

2.4 Create a System Restore Point

For Windows PC's, a system restore point is a snapshot of the internal state of the system at a specific point in time. The restore point will always have a specific date and time attached to the name of the restore point. If a software update or new program installation causes software damage, or a power failure damages a system software file, or there is file damage from other sources, system restore lets you restore your computer's system files to an earlier point in time when the system was working well. The Time Machine utility offers similar functionality for Mac's.

A system restore to an earlier point in time will not affect your data or email stored in the computer.

After doing a tune up, when the computer is running well, is a good time to create a system restore point.

If a virus, or other malware, has infected your computer, a system restore will not get rid of the malware. You must get the rid of the malware first by other means.

However, once the malware is removed, a system restore may undo system software configuration changes done by malware and help restore your computer's operation.

Many times system restores have recovered computers and prevented the expensive and time consuming action of last resort: reformatting the hard drive and reloading all software and data (if the software and data are even available for reloading).

Chapter 3: What's the Cloud and Is It For Me?

For many years, a cloud drawing was used to represent a network. The cloud drawing took care of getting your computer, or server, or whatever device was connected to it, to wherever it needed to go. The cloud/network was omnipresent.

Cloud Computing Concept

More recently, with the emphasis on the applications that omnipresent networks have enabled, the cloud has taken on the meaning of omnipresent software applications and services that run outside of your facility and environment. Of course, you have to have a network connection to get to the cloud, and this is usually the Internet, or a multi-T1 network, depending on what the cloud application or service is.

Basically, clouds offer the advantage of moving complex and expensive hardware and software infrastructures, like server systems, out of the business location and into an offsite location where it will be managed and maintained by the cloud provider. The business doesn't have large upfront capital expenditures (CAPEX) anymore. Instead, the operating expense (OPEX) model is in use where the business uses a shared cloud infrastructure and pays as it goes.

Marketing has used cloud computing to sell hosted services that run the software applications at a remote location. These services are given acronyms like SaaS (Software as a Service), PaaS (Platform as a Service), IaaS (Infrastructure as a Service), HaaS (Hardware as a Service), and even EaaS (Everything as a Service). Users of cloud services access cloud-based applications through their web browser, thin client, or mobile app while the business software and user data is stored on servers at a remote location.

Dropbox, Salesforce.com, and QuickBooks are examples of SaaS. Windows Azure and Google App Engine are examples of PaaS, where businesses use a platform for creating and deploying custom apps, databases and line-of-business services integrated into one platform. With IaaS, businesses purchase infrastructure from providers as virtual resources. Infrastructure components include servers, storage, firewalls, and other components. IaaS providers include Amazon EC2, Rackspace, and Google Compute Engine.

There is more than one kind of cloud. There are private, public, community, and hybrid clouds. A private cloud is a cloud infrastructure operated solely for a single organization. It may be managed by the business or by a third party, and may be physically located at the business or external to the business. The cost is carried by the single organization.

A public cloud is when services are rendered over a network that is open for public use. Security considerations can be very different between private and public clouds. The cost is distributed widely across the public users.

A community cloud shares infrastructure between several organizations from a specific community with common concerns about security, compliance, jurisdiction, etc. It may be managed internally or by a third party, and hosted internally or externally. The cost is distributed across the several organizations.

A hybrid cloud is a composition of private, public, and community clouds.

So, what does all of this mean to you, the small business owner? Most small businesses will likely only need to use Software as a Service (SaaS). With correct choices and implementations, small businesses reap the benefits of not having to deploy expensive and complex IT infrastructures like file and email servers, purchased software running on local servers or computers, or data storage systems. The omnipresent availability of the cloud solutions simplifies collaboration among business partners and local and remote employees over the Internet. Access to sophisticated cloud technology and services usually is possible without putting IT people on the payroll.

Reliable, secure, economically priced offsite data storage has been an established cloud service for some time. There are numerous providers of offsite backup solutions for individual computers as well as servers. Mozy, Carbonite, Intronis, Continuum, and others provide this capability. Of course, you must have reliable Internet access to the cloud. Fortunately, Internet access for the most part is very reliable, although there have been lapses. For example, in 2010, Intuit's site went down for two days. Its small business customers were unable to access their data in Intuit's online offerings including Quicken, QuickBooks and TurboTax.

If you like using Microsoft's Exchange server for mail, Hosted Exchange is an established cloud service. Instead of buying, installing, and managing a Microsoft Exchange server infrastructure, you pay a monthly fee, typically $10-$15/month per user, and access your Exchange server over the Internet.

If you like Microsoft Office products, Office 365 is a cloud-based service that combines Office, SharePoint, Lync and Exchange. Each user pays a monthly fee, typically $5 to $15 per month, depending on the version of Office 365 being used.

Google Apps have been heavily adopted by small businesses, frequently taking the place of onsite server infrastructures. Google Apps is a cloud-based productivity suite that helps people connect and collaboratively get work done from distributed locations using different computing devices. Google Apps includes Gmail, Calendar, Drive, Docs, sheets, and slides. Many small businesses pick and choose, using Google email, Calendar, Docs, and Drive while staying with other Microsoft Office applications.

There are many other applications available as cloud applications spanning document sharing, time billing, project management, forms, document signing, web conferencing, diagram generation, customer resource management (CRM), database platforms, QuickBooks Online, Intuit Online Payroll, expense reports, software training, and others.

Intellis will research cloud services and applications for you, and recommend the best solutions for your business. We will also set up the cloud service and provide administration support as needed.

Finally, a word of caution about cloud applications and services. In the old days of mainframe computers and then mini-computers, users had terminals, not personal computers. The terminals did not have disk drives or high performance processors. The central mainframe or mini-computer did all the computation and ran the software applications. (Does this sound like "cloud computing"?) The business models drove increasing the number of users per centralized computing resource to increase profits. Response times at the terminals could be as long as 4 seconds! This is probably unimaginable to you today, but be aware that as cloud solutions get more and more established, you many want a Quality of Service agreement that guarantees performance and response times.

Precautions

1. Do your homework on a cloud service or application before you sign up for it. How long have they been in business? What reviews are available on Internet searches or Better Business Bureau checks? Do you know anyone using the application you can consult before signing up? Check other references. What support is available from the provider if you have difficulties or questions?
2. As noted earlier, for offsite data backup to the cloud, it's best to use a hybrid approach where a copy of backed up data is kept in an external storage media at your location as well as the backed up data in the cloud.
3. Does the cloud service provider have performance guarantees? Uptime guarantees? Response time guarantees?

Chapter 4: Does My Business Need a Server?

If you do not have a server on your premise, you may have a couple of computers, or a very small number of computers connected in a peer-to-peer network. A peer-to-peer network is where the computers can communicate with each other, any computer can access files on other computers on the network, and any computer can print to a printer connected to the LAN or one of the other computers. A common question is "does my business need a server?"

The basic rule of thumb is, if (a) you have over 5 employees, (b) you and your employees need to work remotely, (c) you are working jointly on shared documents, customer files and records, contracts, photos, publications, etc. with your employees or partners, (d) you need to share confidential documents with partners or customers, (e) you need to share printers and fax machines among employees, and (f) you value high levels of security for your computers, then a server can be a big help for your business. This may be your server on your premise, or a service provider's server-based services in the cloud.

Let's look at the option of purchasing your own server and setting it up on your premise. The advantages are (a) the costs and complexity of server systems have significantly been reduced, (b) all your applications and data are at your business, secure, private, and under your control, (c) you are not dependent on the Internet to access your applications and data, (d) if your server goes down, with the right IT support in place you should be able to get it back up and running quickly – how quickly a cloud provider can get their server-based services back up is less clear, (e) performance of your server should be known and consistent with proper maintenance in place – whether cloud server-based services will maintain performance levels as they add users is unclear, and (f) with the capital equipment (CAPEX) model, you can depreciate your server capital equipment purchase costs and amortize over a multi-year period.

The disadvantages include (a) upfront cost of the server hardware and software infrastructure and installation labor, (b) you will need IT support and server maintenance in place, although for small businesses this does not need to be IT employees – Intellis provides you your IT department at a fraction of the cost, for example , (c) replacement of the server approximately every 5 to 6 years, (d) software upgrade and replacement costs, (e) backup and disaster recovery systems must be in place as part of your server infrastructure.

Now let's look at cloud-based services as an alternative to purchasing your own server.

Some providers of business applications, such as QuickBooks, Enterprise Resource Planning (ERP), Customer Relationship Management (CRM), and other applications have them available through the cloud as Software as a Service (SaaS). The providers run the server infrastructure and hosted applications and you access them through your Internet connection. Your costs are your local Internet infrastructure and pay-as-you-go expenses to the provider.

Google Apps are cloud-based services for email, centralized document storage, and remote access for employees and many small businesses are using these services, rather than using a server on their premise.

Once you have evaluated the pros and cons of having your own server versus using cloud services, and have decided to try the cloud, here are some tips.

Test the waters before jumping in. It is best to start small with a pilot project. This may be having a small number of employees work collaboratively with a Google Docs file, or setting up business gmail for a few employees to try it out. Can the cloud service provider scale up to meet your needs as your business grows? Can you export your data in standard formats, such as Word, Excel, Access, and other programs you use so you can backup and use your data locally if you need to, or move it to another cloud service provider? Is the cloud service provider's contract fair? What is their backup and privacy policy? Are there early termination fees? How do you get your data back if you terminate?

If the cloud providers offer a free trial, try multiple providers out before you choose one.

Chapter 5: What Are Managed Services and Are They For Me?

Before managed services, there was "break/fix". If an IT piece of equipment broke, you called for repair, and someone came to fix it. Of course, this is still necessary today, but the idea of managed services is to keep things from breaking as much as possible. Breakage usually happens at the worst possible time, can cause significant system and employee downtime, can be very expensive, and can really hurt your business. Managed services are designed to head off problems before they get to be big and expensive with a lot of down time. Managed services reduce your IT worries and let you establish a predictable monthly budget for IT expenses.

The centerpiece of Intellis managed services is our proactive 24x7 remote monitoring and management of your computers and servers. Referring to *Chapter 2: Keeping Your Computer Healthy*, we provide complete management of your anti-virus/anti-spyware software and make sure the anti-virus definitions are updating properly, remove temporary files and Internet debris from your hard drive, and remotely monitor the hard drive's health. For example, hard drives with a S.M.A.R.T interface are capable of telling us through this interface that a "disk failure is imminent – back up your data!" We manage software and patch updates remotely, and remotely monitor the offsite backups to make sure the backups are occurring and are successful. If there is a disaster, data recovery is included. We can optionally provide Help Desk services. We can include administration and support for your cloud services in our managed service programs as well.

Intellis managed service programs will keep your computers healthy, and head off problems before they get to be big and expensive with a lot of down time for an affordable, flat-rate monthly fee.

Precautions

1. Does your managed service provider (MSP) offer a full set of managed services which can then be tailored to your particular business? E.g. 24x7 remote monitoring and remediation through a partnership with a professional 24x7 Network Operation Center (NOC), Help Desk support, break/fix services when needed, flat-rate fees, guaranteed response times?
2. Do the people at the Help Desk speak English well enough to effectively support you?
3. Does your MSP provide regular status reports summarizing the results of the remote monitoring and remediation, issues needing action and recommended next steps?

Chapter 6: How Do I Select the Best IT Provider For Me?

With the breadth and complexity of IT, this is not an easy question. IT spans systems, hardware, software, networks, backup and disaster recovery, computers, mobile devices, servers, cloud solutions, security, telephone systems, video surveillance, installation and repair capability, purchase assistance, procurement assistance, project management, vendor management, website development, advice, training, coaching, and mentoring.

The first step is to determine what the IT needs of your business are. You may need "line-of-business" (LOB) software such as specialized accounting software for accounting businesses, or Enterprise Resource Planning (ERP) software for manufacturing businesses. Depending on the software applications, and the size of your business, your hardware may need to be chosen to satisfy your specific business needs. In addition, there will be software applications you will want, such as an accounting program, customer contact management, and others, no matter what kind of business you have.

Do you and your employees require remote communications into your computers or server? Does your email service offer spam protection and enough storage for you? Is your Internet service reliable and fast enough to support your business needs? Is your telephone service reliable with enough features, such as voice mail, call forwarding, etc. to support your business?

Have you identified your security requirements, such as camera video surveillance systems, anti-malware software, anti-spam, and firewalls?

Have you identified the other needed capabilities summarized in *Chapter 1: The Basics That Need To Be In Place*, including summarizing how much data you have to back up, whether there are government requirements on your data management, such as HIPPA, how to protect your data from disaster, and what kind of disaster recovery plans should be in place?

Do you want to have a 24x7 proactive, preventative maintenance plan in place that will keep your computers healthy, as summarized in *Chapter 2: Keeping Your Computers Healthy*, or do you prefer the "if it isn't broken, don't fix it" approach?

Would access to IT professionals with experience and skills in all aspects of IT technology, IT purchasing and procurement, project management, vendor management, website development, advice, training, coaching, and mentoring help you and your business?

A rational decision analysis technique, originally taught by Kepner-Tregoe Associates, calls for listing the criteria for making the decision in rows in the first column in a matrix. The alternatives available are then listed in subsequent columns across the top of the matrix. If there are four alternative solutions being considered, there will be four columns in addition to the criteria column. See the table on the next page. For each cell of the matrix, a short note is entered describing how well the particular alternative satisfies the particular row criteria item. KTA describes an excellent method for numerically quantifying how well each alternative satisfies the criteria, but we have found that just filling in the matrix without the numerical analysis can be a big help to sound, rational decision making.

IT Provider Decision Analysis Matrix

Criteria	Do-It-Yourself, Friend, or Relative	IT Company	Large IT Company	In-house IT Department
Trust & integrity- can they be my trusted IT advisor and partner				
Minimize downtime, loss of productivity				
Time to respond to emergencies and non-emergencies				
Profession-alism-are they timely and professional, do they take other calls on my time				

Backup & disaster recovery solutions				
24x7 proactive preventative maintenance & monitoring, flat-rate solutions				
Help Desk option				
Detailed, thorough proposals, quotes				
Clear communications in terms I can understand; do they listen to me				
Thoroughness – do I have confidence they will do a complete job; do they document their work				
Follow up – do they report results, status, and follow up with me				
Breadth and depth of IT knowledge & experience				
Breadth of services offered				

Willingness to tailor their solutions to my specific needs				
Assistance in IT planning, purchasing, project & vendor management, advising				
Strong references				
Overall cost for my business				

Do-It Yourself, Friend, or Relative

Many small businesses start with this type of IT support. The owner may be tech savvy, or has a friend or family member who will help. However, it usually doesn't take very long before (a) the owner, friend, or relative can't provide the timeliness that is required, or (b) more technical depth and breadth is required.

Pluses	Minuses
- IT support hourly rate may be lower	- Overall cost to the business may be high
	- Owner may need to spend time on business, not IT issues
	- Friend or relative may not be available when critically needed
	- Owner, friend, or relative may not have the technical skills or experience

IT Company

There are many IT companies, of various sizes, who would like you to trust them with your IT support. If the IT company has grown to the Large IT Company size, we'll discuss the pros and cons below. For the rest, the key question is are they managed well enough, and have the quality of staff, to provide the excellent technical support and timeliness you require.

The quality of the management and technical expertise of these companies will vary considerably. The interpersonal skills of the owners and technicians can vary considerably as well. The Decision Analysis Matrix will provide a criteria for evaluating these companies.

For a well-managed IT company with strong technical staff with good interpersonal skills there are many advantages.

Pluses	Minuses
- Cost savings over hiring your own IT people	- Loss of control
- Breadth of IT management and technical skills available to you that would be difficult to hire	- Possibility of confidentiality and security breaches
-Allows you to spend time on your business, not IT issues	- Possibility of data loss
- Your IT technology can help your business, not hinder it	

Large IT Company

Many large IT companies have larger companies as clients. If the Large IT Company is well-managed with excellent management and technical staff, they can still do a good job with the smaller clients. However, the Large IT Company's larger clients frequently get priority. As a small business owner, this is a significant concern.

Pluses	Minuses
- More technical staff	- Hourly rate can be higher than smaller IT companies
- Breadth of IT management and technical skills available to you that would be difficult to hire	- Loss of control
-Allows you to spend time on your business, not IT issues	- Possibility of confidentiality and security breaches
- Your IT technology can help your business, not hinder it	- Possibility of data loss
	-Timeliness of response; lower priority service
	- Less personal interaction; more ticketing, etc.

In-house IT Department

Just like many companies have their own marketing or customer service departments, they create IT departments. Usually, they do this because they want the control and direct management that results from having this department in-house. Establishing and managing an IT department is a challenging task. Skilled, experienced IT professionals are expensive. Because of the breadth of IT technology, multiple IT people are required. IT technology changes so rapidly that on-going technical education is required for the IT people.

Let's look at what an IT department usually does.

- Provide technology strategic and tactical direction and plans
- Technology budgets and plans
- Provide technical security and protection for the business
- Provide protection and disaster recovery for business data
- Specify and install new software and equipment
- Repair equipment
- Emergency response
- Answer employee questions and help them with technology
- Train employees on technology

There is a significant span of core competencies required. Usually, multiple people are required to cover this span. One person will rarely have the breadth and depth of skills and experience.

If the IT department has implemented preventative maintenance systems and practices, there will not need to be as many IT people on the staff. The total cost of ownership is lower when equipment is regularly maintained and replaced at end of life. Unfortunately, most departments are not motivated by reducing their size, and the tendency is for IT departments to continually grow.

Pluses	Minuses
- More direct control	- Breadth of IT management and technical skills that must be hired
	- More expense; salaries, payroll taxes and benefits
	- Tendency for IT departments to continually grow in size

The Case for Outsourcing Your IT Support

Outsourcing your IT support to an outside company that operates as "your IT Department at a fraction of the cost" can be the best solution for your business.

Cost Savings

An IT professional you hire at $65,000/year salary is really costing you an additional $19,500/year in payroll taxes and benefits, and when you factor in vacation, business holidays, training, and other non-productive time, the total cost of this person is $93,641/year. These costs don't include the expensive hardware and software IT professionals often need, floor space, phones, and other equipment.

The core competencies of a typical IT department span desktop, laptop, and mobile devices, servers, local and wide area networks, security, backup and disaster recovery, web programming, telephone systems, technology strategic and tactical planning and budgeting, and IT best practices. It will probably take at least 3 to 4 different people to provide all of this breadth of coverage, but the size of your business may not require 120 to 160 hours per week of IT support.

If you aren't big enough to consistently keep at least 3 to 4 IT people busy full time, you should outsource.

Furthermore, when preventative maintenance and 24x7 remote monitoring and management programs are properly implemented, the need for dedicated IT employees is decreased significantly and the case for outsourcing becomes even stronger.

Time Savings

As a business owner, you want to spend your time on moving the business forward and making your company more productive, more efficient, and more profitable. You want your employees to do the same. Time spent on IT problems, "waiting on the computer", and slow responding systems hurts your business. A professional outsourced IT company can take care of your technical infrastructure and keep you focused on your business.

Mitigation of Minuses

A well-managed, professional IT company should be able to earn your trust as your trusted technology partner, and put controls and systems in place that will secure and protect your confidential information and data. By operating as if they were your IT department, you will maintain control at a fraction of the cost.

Appendix A: Definitions

access point	A device that provides a Wi-Fi wireless network without routing of computer and device network addresses.
anti-spam	Methods to detect and send unsolicited messages and advertisements to a junk filter.
anti-virus	Methods to detect and send malicious software to a quarantine folder, or eliminate the virus altogether.
attachment	A file that is sent along with an e-mail message. ASCII (plain text) can be appended to the message text. Other types of files must be encoded (MIME, BinHex, and Uuencode formats)
backup	Copies of information such as files, images, programs, databases, and other data that are made so lost, corrupted, or deleted data can be recovered.
bandwidth	The data throughput capacity of a network. The higher the bandwidth, the higher the volume of data that can be transmitted. For networks, bandwidth is typically measured in bits per second (bps). Bytes per second may sometimes be used (Bps). 1 Byte equals 8 bits.
bit	A binary (base-2 arithmetic) digit with the value of zero or one. It is the most basic unit of data that a computer works with.

bot	Short for robot. Hackers can insert malicious software into a computer to make it follow the commands of the hacker. These commands are typically used to broadcast spam, viruses, attack web sites, and do other malicious actions.
bot net	This is a group of hacked bot computers (a "zombie army") with malicious software inserted so they follow the malicious commands of the hacker.
byte	A group of 8 binary digits, or bits that comprises a computer "word".
citrix	A software and services company that provides licenses for virtualization and remote access software for delivering applications over a network and the Internet.
client	A program or computer that connects to and communicates with a server. Client programs may also be referred to as "client software", or "client-server software".
cloud	A commonly used shorthand for a cloud provided service or application, or the aggregation of all cloud services and applications..."The Cloud".
cloud computing	A generic term describing Internet services such as social network services (Facebook and Twitter), online backup services, and applications that run within a Web browser. Cloud computing also refers to computer networks that are connected over the Internet for cluster computing or server redundancy purposes.

colocation	A colocation (or colo) is an offsite location that stores an organization's data and backups.
cookie	A small piece of information your computer may be asked to accept when connecting to certain servers via a web browser. The browser stores the cookie in a text file. A cookie is specific to the server that sent it, and is only used for communication with that server.
disaster recovery	Plans and procedures for recovery or continuation of technology infrastructure critical to a business after a disaster.
DSL	Digital Subscriber Loop communications line. This is a widely implemented method of connecting to the Internet over telephone twisted-pair lines.
encryption	The translation of data into a secret code created with the use of an encryption key. Once encrypted, you cannot retrieve the data without the key.
ethernet	A common communication network technology that allows data to travel up to gigabit (10^9 bits/sec) speeds.
firewall	A hardware, software, or both system to prevent unauthorized access to or from a particular network. All messages entering or leaving the Intranet passing through the firewall are inspected and messages that do not pass the security criteria are blocked.

fragmentation	The scattering of parts of the same disk file over different physical areas of a disk surface. Fragmentation occurs as files are deleted and new ones are added.
gigabyte	Gig's or GB. Approximately one billion bytes or 1000 megabytes.
IaaS	Infrastructure as a Service. Providers of IaaS offer computer and server infrastructures, physical and virtual, in the most basic cloud-service model.
IP Address	Internet Protocol address. There are "public-facing" IP addresses and private, or LAN, IP addresses. Every computer connected to the Internet has an IP address. E.g. 192.168.0.100, which is a LAN IP address.
ISP	Internet Service Provider. This is the organization or company that provides Internet connectivity and access.
Kbps	Kilobits per second, or Kbps. One Kbps is 1000 bits per second.
LAN	Local Area Network. A network that extends over a small area, typically a square mile or less. Computers and other network devices are connected together over the LAN for the purpose of sharing resources such as files, data, programs, or printers.
main memory	The amount of physical memory installed in your computer, sometimes referred to as RAM (random access memory).

malware	malicious software programs designed to damage, corrupt, or do other unwanted actions on a computer. Examples are viruses, worms, Trojan horses, and spyware.
megabyte	Meg's or MB. One MB equals one million bytes.
MHz or mhz	Megahertz, the unit of a processor's speed. One MHz equals one million cycles per second. This speed determines how many instructions per second a processor can execute. Generally, the higher the number of MHz, the faster the computer.
NAT	Network Address Translation. A security standard that enables a LAN to use a set of private IP address for internal traffic and a single public-facing IP address for communications with the Internet. NAT is typically performed by the router.
network	a group of interconnected computers exchanging information.
network monitoring	A cloud-based network monitoring service can configure and remotely monitor all computers, servers, and systems (servers, computes, routers, available disk space, backup applications, critical virus detection, and more)
NOC	Network Operations Center. A location, usually remote, where network monitoring and remediation of computers, servers, routers, anti-malware operation, backup results, available disk space, and more occurs. NOC's typically operate 24x7.

offsite storage	Storage of data in a separate location from where the business is located. Professional offsite storage locations typically employ redundancy, emergency power generators, and encryption to protect user's data.
PaaS	Platform as a service. Cloud providers provide a computing platform that typically includes an operating system, programming language execution environment, database, and web server.
patch	This is a software update. Most software requires patches to ensure continuing security protection and fix defects in the software.
peer-to-peer	A type of network connection between computers where data and other information is communicated. There is no hierarchy as there is with a client-server connection where one computer makes a request and the other responds with information.
phishing	A scam that scammers use to electronically collect personal information such as social security numbers, credit card information, user logon and password credentials, and other personal information from unsuspecting users. Phishers typically send authentic looking emails that appear to come from legitimate websites such as eBay, PayPal, banks, government institutions, FedEx, and other sources asking you to click on a link included in the email and then update or validate your personal information.

private cloud	Private cloud, also called internal cloud or corporate cloud, refers to a proprietary computing architecture that provides hosted services to a limited number of users.
RAM	Random Access Memory is the system, or main memory in a computer. This memory is faster than disk memory. A typical computer may have 4 GB (4000 million bytes) of RAM.
remote desktop	A Windows capability that allows you to have access to a Windows session in another computer in a different location.
router	A networking device that forwards data packets from one network to another. Routers can filter packets and forward them according to a specified criteria.
Saas	Software as a Service is a software delivery model where software and associated data is centrally hosted in the cloud. SaaS is typically accessed by users using a web browser.
server	A computer that is responsible for responding to requests made by a client computer or client program. File servers manage files, print servers manage printers, and email servers manage email. There are also specialty servers that host a specific application(s).
spam	The electronic equivalent of junk mail. Spammers collect email addresses from chat rooms, websites, customer lists, newsgroups, and viruses which harvest users' address books, and are sold to other spammers.

spyware	Any software that secretly gathers user information, usually for advertising purposes, through the user's Internet connection.
T-1 carrier	A dedicated telephone line connection with 1.544 Mbps of downstream and upstream bandwidth. Usually, T-1 connections carry both voice and data communications. T-1 lines are sometimes used for businesses to connect to the Internet and for Internet Service Providers to connect to the Internet backbone network. A T-1 line is sometimes referred to as DS1 line.
T-3 carrier	A dedicated telephone line connection with approximately 43 Mbps of bandwidth. T-3 lines are mainly used by Internet Service Providers to connect to the Internet backbone and for the backbone network itself. A T-3 line is sometimes referred to as a DS3 line.
terminal services	Terminal services, known as Remote Desktop Connection from Windows Server 2008 R2 and later, allow a remote user to access applications and data on a remote computer over a network. The load on the network is reduced because only mouse clicks, keyboard clicks, and video screens are communicated over the network.
URL	Universal Resource Locator. This is a way of locating resources on the Internet when it is entered in URL field in your browser. E.g. the URL for Yahoo is http://www.yahoo.com.
virtualization	Virtualization is the creation of a virtual, rather than an actual, version of a hardware platform, operating system, storage device or network resource.

VPN	Virtual Private Network. A VPN emulates a direct, secure point-to-point connection across an unsecured public (e.g. Internet) or private network. Data is encrypted and encapsulated with routing information as it travels the unsecured networks to prevent hacking and deciphering. VPN connections allow people to work at home with all the network connectivity and services they have in their office.
WAN	Wide Area Network. A group of networked computers covering a large geographical area such as the Internet.
Wi-Fi	Wireless Fidelity or a wireless network. This is a general term from the Wi-Fi Alliance that refers to any type of IEEE 802.11 a/b/g/n network. Products approved as "Wi-Fi Certified" (a registered trademark) are certified to interoperate with each other for wireless communications.

IT SOLUTIONS FOCUSED ON YOUR BUSINESS

First, we listen to your needs and understand your business requirements. Then we determine what technologies and solutions best match these needs so that you can work more productively, profitably, and securely.

YOUR TRUSTED IT PARTNER

Other companies offer tech support when things break. We offer premier tech support and far more - strategic and tactical direction, technical expertise, and the kind of guidance and help that only comes from a trusted IT partner.

Jim Hood, Owner & President

INTELLIS

jhood@intellis-tech.com

www.intellis-tech.com

Please Contact Me Regarding the Following

Free Business Guides

- ☐ A Business Guide for Protecting Sensitive Information
- ☐ Intellis Company Brochure
- ☐ Intellis Managed Services
- ☐ Intellis Help Desk
- ☐ The 10 Most Important Reasons Why You Should Choose Intellis to Support Your Computer Network
- ☐ FREE Computer Health Checkup Brochure
- ☐ FREE Computer Technology Assessment Brochure

Free Technology Assessments

I Need Help With the Following: ____________________

____

____

____

Name: ____________________

Company: ____________________

Email: ____________________

Phone: ____________________

Address: ____________________

Send To: INTELLIS
P.O. Box 2068
Petaluma, CA 94953
jhood@intellis-tech.com

Made in the USA
Monee, IL
04 November 2026

67378652R00036